NEW CALIFORNIA POETRY

edited by	Robert Hass
	Calvin Bedient
	Brenda Hillman
	Forrest Gander

For, by Carol Snow

Enola Gay, by Mark Levine

Selected Poems, by Fanny Howe

Sleeping with the Dictionary, by Harryette Mullen

Commons, by Myung Mi Kim

The Guns and Flags Project, by Geoffrey G. O'Brien

Gone, by Fanny Howe

Why / Why Not, by Martha Ronk

A Carnage in the Lovetrees, by Richard Greenfield

The Seventy Prepositions, by Carol Snow

Not Even Then, by Brian Blanchfield

Facts for Visitors, by Srikanth Reddy

Weather Eye Open, by Sarah Gridley

Subject, by Laura Mullen

This Connection of Everyone with Lungs, by Juliana Spahr

The Totality for Kids, by Joshua Clover

The Wilds, by Mark Levine

I Love Artists, by Mei-mei Berssenbrugge

Harm., by Steve Willard

Green and Gray, by Geoffrey G. O'Brien

The Age of Huts (compleat), by Ron Silliman

Selected Poems, 1974–2006: it's go in horizontal, by Leslie Scalapino

rimertown / an atlas, by Laura Walker

Ours, by Cole Swensen

Virgil and the Mountain Cat, by David Lau

Sight Map, by Brian Teare

Transcendental Studies: A Trilogy, by Keith Waldrop

R's Boat, by Lisa Robertson

Green is the Orator, by Sarah Gridley

Writing the Silences, by Richard O. Moore

Writing the Silences

RICHARD O. MOORE

Writing the Silences

EDITED BY Brenda Hillman and Paul Ebenkamp
FOREWORD BY Brenda Hillman

 University of California Press   Berkeley   Los Angeles   London

University of California Press, one of the most distinguished university presses in the United States, enriches lives around the world by advancing scholarship in the humanities, social sciences, and natural sciences. Its activities are supported by the UC Press Foundation and by philanthropic contributions from individuals and institutions. For more information, visit www.ucpress.edu.

University of California Press
Berkeley and Los Angeles, California

University of California Press, Ltd.
London, England

Frontispiece: Richard O. Moore, Venice, Italy, 1978. Photo by Barbara Van Dyke.

LIBRARY OF CONGRESS CATALOGING-IN-PUBLICATION DATA
Moore, Richard O.
    Writing the silences / Richard O. Moore ; edited by Brenda Hillman and Paul Ebenkamp ; foreword by Brenda Hillman.
        p.   cm. — (New California poetry ; 30)
    ISBN 978-0-520-26243-0 (cloth : alk. paper)
    ISBN 978-0-520-26244-7 (pbk. : alk. paper)
    I. Hillman, Brenda.   II. Ebenkamp, Paul.   III. Title.

PS3613.O5666W75   2010
811'.6—dc22

                                        2009032807

Manufactured in the United States of America

19   18   17   16   15   14   13   12   11   10
10   9   8   7   6   5   4   3   2   1

The paper used in this publication meets the minimum requirements of ANSI/NISO Z39.48-1992 (R 1997) (Permanence of Paper).

For Flinn, David, Lisa, Michael, Anthony, Aran

Contents

Photographs follow page 96

ix *Foreword*
Brenda Hillman

xix *Acknowledgments*

POEMS 1960–2008

3 [Therefore, set forth over the black river]

5 Shadow and Light

6 Itinerary

7 By the Lake

8 Utensils

9 Driving to Fort Bragg

10 Dog in the Forest

11 History

13 Columbia 1960

15 Ten Philosophical Asides

27 Marginalia: Whitehead

28 Quotations

30 Analects

33 *from* d e l e t e

41 "Come Live with Me"

42 : It :

43 *from* Writing the Silences

51 "Come Sunday"

52 Birthright

55 Notebook

56 This Morning

57 Aftershock

58 Visiting Hours

60 The Parachutist's Annunciation

63 Holding On

73 *...a divertimento...*

74 Footnotes

76 A Funeral of Memory

77 The Winter Garden

82 A Treasury of Darkness

83 Introit

84 Over the Shoulder

85 Meanwhile

POEMS 1946–1957

89 *from* A History Primer

90 Seascape

91 *from* September Elegy

92 *from* At Caesar's Gate

94 A Reminiscence

95 Birthday View Opening on a Garden

107 *Notes*

Foreword

About a decade ago, a quiet man by the name of Richard O. Moore who looked to be in his seventies signed up for my class at a writers' conference. I was struck by the intensity of his poetry, by its philosophical meditations. We talked about Buddhism and Gnosticism, about language and interiority, non-being, the insides of words, about silence and about "the thing," about the impossibility ever of reaching "it." We talked about the concrete words for the concept of "nothingness" that Kierkegaard had introduced with such material force—"the void," "the abyss"—words that now settle into utter paradox with a Heideggerian twist and a textured absence. He was interested in Wittgenstein and language theory, in modernist quandaries of liminal states of feeling, and he wrote of the conjunction of idea and language as material but not purely abstractly or theoretically. It was a quest. His reading and interests were not the usual fare of a writers' conference. I asked him about his writing life; he had been writing a long time, he said, but had only been working on the poems at hand for about ten years or so. His manner was modest and self-effacing; he was (and is) nearly incapable of accepting praise. Because I was engaged by his quest, by the variety of the work and by the mental life reflected there, I felt determined to follow his progress.

Our exchanges continued after the conference; he was living up in Point Arena at the time, and we corresponded through several changes in his life—the loss of his wife, several moves. I read everything he sent me with pleasure, sometimes offering editorial suggestions. Poetry seems to sort itself into work one would not want to read again and work one would want to read again, and Moore's poetry belonged to the second category. Because he hadn't told me anything about himself I had the idea that this fellow had always worked in intense isolation on the foggy coast of Northern California.

A few years after those early exchanges, I realized the Richard O. Moore I knew was the Richard Moore who had belonged to the group known as the San Francisco Renaissance poets. I came across his name while rereading Michael Davidson's fascinating study, *The San Francisco Renaissance.* I found out Moore was born in Ohio in 1920, attended the University of California at Berkeley in the late 1930s, and had first studied poetry under the tutelage of Josephine Miles, developing an ear for efficient meters and for subtle ironies. One can see the influence of Miles's careful measures in the early work collected here. The poetry from that period is often bardic, with a sweeping symbolism; the sections of "A History Primer" and "At Caesar's Gate" also show the influence of Yeats.

Moore has noted he can't remember when he first heard about Kenneth Rexroth's literary salons, but in the late 1930s (when they were still students), he and Tom Parkinson traveled across the Bay to attend "the Fridays"—as well as meetings of the Anarchist-Libertarian Circle—at the home of Kenneth and Marie Rexroth on Potrero Hill. These gatherings are documented both in Davidson's study and in Linda Hamalian's biography of Rexroth. When asked what the Fridays consisted of in the early days, Moore replied, "What they always consisted of: whatever was on Kenneth's mind at the time."

The legendary group was also from its inception open to people Rexroth invited in a spontaneous fashion; Moore has noted wryly, "It was not so much about who was invited but about who hadn't been kicked out!" Grounded in anarchist-pacifist principles, the group included political activists, poets, visual artists and friends of the Rexroths. Over the next decades, it grew to include not only Moore and Parkinson but also—on occasion— poets Helen Adam, James Broughton, Robert Duncan, William Everson, Madeline Gleason, Philip Lamantia, James Laughlin, Jack Spicer and Philip Whalen, among others, as well as poets later associated with the Beat Movement: Allen Ginsberg, Michael McClure and Gary Snyder. Marthe Rexroth Whitcomb, Rexroth's third wife, has noted in conversation that some of the early participants of the group were "Italian chicken-farmer anarchists from Petaluma." At one point, William Carlos Williams dropped by when he was in town. During one period, the Friday group also met for a time at Richard Moore's apartment at the corner of Post and Mason.

From his earliest days at Berkeley, Moore was drawn to the formal study of philosophy; he became a pacifist. As World War II started, he stopped working on his degree, attracted by the ideals of political activism, and began to pursue dance and poetry. Moore tells a story (recounted at greater length in Matthew Lasar's *Pacifica Radio: The Rise of an Alternative Network*) of how, when he was ordered to report for an interview for military service in the early 1940s, he was asked what he did for a living. "I'm a poet," he replied. The officer asked: "What do you really do?" Moore replied: "I'm a ballet dancer." This caused consternation. When asked whether he could follow orders, Moore said, "It depends on what they are." The officer dismissed him from military service, giving him a 4-F classification with a medical diagnosis of "psychotic neurotic"—a term referred to in his poem "Birthright"—after which he became an advisor to others on war resistance, non-compliance, and attaining conscientious objector status.

Moore's poetry came to be haunted by images of barren landscapes and resistance to violence. Often in his poems—for example, in the sequence called "Holding On"—this resistance has to do with negotiating silences, with a responsibility to accuracy and with a refusal to make easy gestures. A poet's struggle is in relation to meaning itself, the idea of meaning in a world that has no easy gods or moral codes, a world in which institutions refuse to cooperate. Such resistance—and the provisions made by the mind in relation to non-human nature—are the main motifs and methods of this volume.

The twinning of political resistance and art practice was, of course, characteristic of many writers of the Rexroth circle. Enraged by Naziism, Stalinism and bourgeois liberalism alike, Rexroth himself developed what Hamalian describes as "disaffiliation from 'the American capitalist state, and from the State as such,'" believing that a "social order built on anarcho-pacifism could nurture the free development of the self" (p. 114). This stance offered vast inspiration for the iconoclastic writers who worked under his sway at the edge of the continent, away from the established intellectual communities of the East Coast. Rexroth's energetic, rebellious, anti-authoritarian, free-wheeling style—however full of "hot air" at times—captivated many who knew him, and he captivated Moore, who has detailed memories of his up-and-down relationship with Rexroth, as both an acolyte and a friend. ("A Reminiscence" records one aspect of this friendship in delicately rhymed quatrains, describing a walk in autumn along the Russian River in the 1940s.) Moore developed an eclectic style apart from Rexroth's, foregrounding the materials of language in the wrestling match with silence.

It was also a time of "firsts" for poetry performance. As I write this Preface, there are dozens of poetry readings each week in the Bay Area; but just a few decades back, San Francisco did not have many literary readings, and there were no "group readings" until Madeline Gleason organized her famous readings in a San Francisco art gallery. The first reader at the first event on April 22, 1947, was Richard Moore. Of this historic occasion, Ron Silliman has noted in his blog:

> [T]he April 1947 "First Festival of Modern Poetry," organized by Gleason at the Lucien Labaudt Gallery on Gough Street in San Francisco—12 poets reading over a period of two days—was the first event of its kind, perhaps anywhere, and certainly an important antecedent not only to the [San Francisco State] Poetry Center, but to the Six Gallery reading in 1955 where Allen Ginsberg first read "Howl," and beyond. (February 22, 2006)

After the war, Moore seems to have pushed against the coterie atmosphere of exclusionary poetics. He was interested in writers of many and often divergent aesthetic dispositions, and he tried not to narrow himself. He never wanted to toe any party line but wanted instead to read and incorporate many influences, to be as eclectic as he possibly could be, to regard no group of writers as arbiters, gods or judges. His work of the 1950s and 1960s shows affinities with that of Everson, Duncan and Spicer (and of other western writers, particularly Jeffers) but also of more "establishment" writers. Captivated by arguments about language in the 1980s, he did not eschew psychological struggle as a feature. In poems like "The Parachutist's Annunciation" the reader will note the hybrid styles. He moved increasingly to philosophical and linguistic interrogation and skepticism. The poems of natural description—"Driving to Fort Bragg," for example—are set against a backdrop of the untamed Northern California coast where he mostly made his home, but refer speculatively to time and history. He kept up with the work of his early group of poets over the years and has said, in his characteristically quiet manner, "I am the last of my kind."

■

Later, Richard Moore was to make a successful career in the worlds of alternative radio, television and film. With Lewis Hill and Eleanor McKinney, he participated in the founding of Pacifica Radio, the first non-profit public radio station in the country. Much has been written about the importance of Pacifica Radio, a listener-supported public station that provided a forum for free expression, especially in the areas of social justice and literary and performing arts. The founders were determined to oppose American militarism and imperialism and to promote progressive cultural change. Matthew Lasar's book has an excellent account of this important period of cultural history; Moore has said, "That is a whole separate chapter."

During these decades working in other media, Moore developed a signature style of poetry: open, spare verse that foregrounds philosophical enquiry. His poetry reflects aspects of his involvement with the collective consciousness and the idea of language as the intersection of private and public space. His poetry has continued to reflect the values and eclectic free-verse styles of the San Francisco Renaissance writers: a growing interest in experimental lyric; a blend of traditional rhymes with very relaxed, unfettered prose-poetry ("Columbia 1960"); fresh forms of personal address; and a growing interest in the philosophy of language as subject matter and in method. Possibly the concern for language as the link between outer and inner haunted him because of his work with public radio; as an instrument of change, radio operated in the interstices between public and private, social and commercial. From KPFA and cutting-edge alternative radio, Moore became a member of the staff of KQED. David Stewart writes of this move:

> At KQED, [Moore] soon became a TV producer and an accomplished filmmaker. As a poet he had been associated with Kenneth Rexroth's anarchist libertarian group. "Coming to KQED in 1952 was my version of going straight," he says. (*Current,* February 3, 1997)

Moore said he never stopped thinking of himself as a poet. For the next several decades, he devoted himself "on the surface" to the arts, spiritual practices and political presentations of other writers, making hundreds of programs for public television that included a huge range of poets: John Ashbery, Robert Creeley, Robert Duncan, Randall Jarrell, Frank O'Hara, Anne Sexton, and Louis Zukofsky, among others. At KPFA, he also started a series on eastern religious thought, hosted by Alan Watts, which he later imported to public television. Among other innovative programs was an hour-long collaboration between Merce Cunningham and John Cage.

His professional life as a business person working for non-profit networks involved many life changes—some gradual and some sudden. He spent the entirety of the 1980s in Minnesota at KTCA, and one can see in the poetry of this period an experimental and perhaps even lonely turn. Through several family configurations—including a long marriage to Ruth McNerny Moore—he continued to balance the challenges of being an adept organizer and manager with the skills of a poet. After his retirement from public network management, he returned west and lived in several parts of California before settling in Marin County. Since the 1980s, he has been highly prolific and seems to have devoted himself to his writing with increasing intensity.

It's baffling to understand why Richard Moore published so little along the way. Other writers in his cohort were not hesitant at all. He was certainly hard at work promoting the work of others. His first official publication seems to have been in the famed but short-lived *Ark* magazine, which Linda Hamalian describes thus:

> The magazine has a decided pacifist and anti-state position; . . . Its first and only issue (spring 1947) included Rexroth's "Advent 1947" and works by William Everson, Robert Duncan, Thomas Parkinson, Richard Moore, Kenneth Patchen, James Laughlin, Richard Eberhart, British anarchist George Woodcock, Paul Goodman, e e cummings, Robert Stock and William Carlos Williams. (*A Life of Kenneth Rexroth,* p. 153)

In such company, one would think the young poet would develop a great deal of confidence. In the next few decades, he published occasionally when asked: twice in the old avant-garde *Circle* magazine, several times in *The Formalist,* several times in *Talisman.* And if he has pursued publication rarely and reluctantly, he also has kept track of his pieces rather haphazardly; during the assembly of this volume, Paul Ebenkamp and I were repeatedly amused that scraps of early poems kept turning up and copies kept being faxed from many different places as his children heard about our project.

■

Finally, like many of the San Francisco poets of his generation, Richard Moore has been informed by regional and ecological concerns; a commitment to freshness and freedom of form and expression; a foregrounding of language as material in itself; the inclusion of leftist politics and issues of social justice; an exploration of spiritual and philosophical matters that reflect a blend of Buddhist and antinomian western thought; and an excitement about the performative aspects of the poetry. Michael Davidson elucidates these values quite fruitfully. Moore has taken these values in his own direction; for example, the features of his western regional pieces are often subject to a different kind of philosophical distancing than Philip Whalen's or Gary Snyder's work, but like theirs, his work is bound by praise for the nonhuman: "high on the lifting thermals, / a slim hawk, / the wing tips keep / bold balance on the blind / push of air," he writes in "September Elegy." This volume shows the unfolding of these qualities over six decades.

The feature of his writing that resonates most for me is what drew me to his work in our first meeting; it is a seriousness and intensity that is rare now in poetry, and it reminds me of Duncan and Yeats, of the bardic task. His arguments with silence pressure the words to come forth, to come to terms with themselves. In "Writing the Silences," the poet implores the white spaces to speak to one another—the two columns to "cross over" the large gap:

a word I	the appearance of
is enough	to shrink the world
there will be	no coffee
following silence	no

The meditations in this group of poems track consciousness and language in a careful and somewhat abstract manner, building two columns with a spare and tensile strength. Like many poets interested in the intersections of avant-garde writing and its sisters, Moore sought to keep his writing informed by the best traditions of his time; he was a great fan of Elizabeth Bishop and Louis Zukofsky, even as he kept up with Duncan and read the experimental writers of the 1980s, approaching the issues of the isolated materials of language as a student of Buddhism, pacifism and Wittgenstein. There is often an intensely psychological and personal struggle resonating at the core of his work.

Recently I was rereading Moore's poem "A Funeral of Memory," which addresses memory in terms that are drawn from existentialist philosophy and drama, mathematics, religious inquiry:

I say "Enter, thin needle of infinite night."
and so it is   the set is overfull

calling on god I enter the set called silence

once in the labyrinth   old alley of no exit
there is only the center and the deception of place
here everything happens and nothing is foretold

The word "set" is the poem's most flexible term: a set as a collection that can be added to, a set as a gathering that is already fixed and complete, a set as a scene for a movie—all are suggested here. The "set" of philosophical associations Richard Moore offers is simultaneously general, deep, orphic, prophetic and unconcerned. His poems speak to me repeatedly of the search he has been involved in for over sixty years of writing—a search through language for language, in language and to the side of language—for a kind of silence that is eerie, immeasurable, sacred, populated, organic, special and at one with its own process of meaning-making.

Brenda Hillman
2009

SOURCES

Michael Davidson, *The San Francisco Renaissance: Poetics and Community at Mid-Century,* Cambridge: Cambridge University Press, 1989

Linda Hamalian, *A Life of Kenneth Rexroth,* New York: Norton, 1991

Matthew Lasar, *Pacifica Radio: The Rise of an Alternative Network,* Philadelphia: Temple University Press, 2000

Ron Silliman, http://ronsilliman.blogspot.com, accessed February 22, 2006

David Stewart, "KQED Made Its Mark by Making Programs," *Current,* February 3, 1997

Marthe Rexroth Whitcomb, personal interviews, 2007–2008

Acknowledgments

Some of these poems have appeared in the following periodicals:

"Ten Philosophical Asides," excerpts: *Poetry USA,* 1994

"Writing the Silences": *The Redwood Coast Review,* 1997

"This Morning": *Independent Coast Observer,* 1992

"Holding On": *Talisman,* no. 12, Spring 1994

"A History Primer": *Circle,* no. 9, July 1946

"Seascape": *Poetry* 67, no. 4, January 1946

"September Elegy": *The Formalist* 1, no. 2, Autumn 1949

Without the encouragement, editorial judgment, and, finally, loving persistence of Brenda Hillman, this selection of poems would have never been assembled and submitted to a publisher. I am deeply grateful for her guiding hand throughout the entire process.

Also, thanks are due Paul Ebenkamp for the hours spent in assembling and typing the poems, some from faded scraps of paper. I also appreciate his editorial input.

POEMS 1960–2008

[Therefore, set forth over the black river]

Death is not to be turned toward nor
Is it a breathing presence at the neck.
Death must be made in the language of life.

A wide word span, a random dream game
A virtual space in our smalltalk, as with:

"To enter [why not like a bird?] a great hall."

Shadow and Light

Incised in concrete
knife-edged shadow
frond a perfect
arrest of clarity

a palm frond arrow
from a declining sun

shadow and light
lust of epiphany
the illusion that walks
with me on concrete

invisible come-along
shadow and light

epiphany of the shadow
tangible as light palm shape
holds me timeless until
without thinking I pass by

an arrest of clarity held
and released by a declining
sun : step over the shadow
light vanishes a passerby

Itinerary

Monologues of white interiors
time-dried of water and wind

crowds gather in history's emptiness
weightless in the hollows of memory

description without witness
so long ago lost.

By the Lake

Past years are figures in old glass
wobbly in a lake
wrinkled by a stone.

The lake will settle down
a face will reappear
in a scent of evergreen.

Years are present as noon as now
or in a rippled moonglade night;
they summon shadow as in fragile memory
easy as stepping into a lake
breaking the present mirror.

It is the way events are stored,
they come back twisted
in wrinkles of water

blurred inscapes into today.

Utensils

An available palette thickened by air
words I hold and so fast lose.

A thunder so low   an inaudible present   its slow
cycles place me shaking in its throat.

Stare   and beauty opens like a work of fire
a made thing   a connection must be made.

This is to say necessity is a place made all of stares
come beauty   come the final ruin of the world. Stop :

for what it may be   or was   a burned-in-after-flash of fire
over distance measured light years. The glamour of it all.

Driving to Fort Bragg

"... the existence of the appearance is the reality
in question ..."
JOHN SEARLE

Inferred only *this* time *is* history, yet uncovered:

hawks on fence posts, even ravens those acrobats, fog
has called a general strike along the coast, no
thermal-lazing, hovering, no tidying-up by vultures
descended from above;

through cataracts dimly, once winged enterprise,
feathers tented against rain, these vision-
masters of the air ... headlights
catch them in refracting dawn;
whatever their hunger the ceiling will not yield,
bird shapes lost in the moment of discovery,
as if light, after millennia released, reduced substance to ash,
a part of the vast curriculum of circumstance and nothing,
with yesterday's blinding sunlight withheld there,
so many questions fearful to be asked;

place *this* with the pacific fence post
posturing of hawks.

Dog in the Forest

A city in ruins   as ever.

In the forest every scent comes arrowing true,
a "state of exception"   where the air opens up to death
as everyone's property   thrown in the corner
a loose rag   "the ultimate configuration of facts."

When we were young and feral
we made paths into the city
a sanctuary   with doors and corridors.

Then were promises and obligations kept
like subway tokens against uncertainty.

There were nights that continued ecstatic to morning,
in the red of your hair dawn sprinkled you with diamond light.

Can it be told when an ancient trace of faith
gave way under stress   in every modern word?

Running through a melancholy of photographs and kitchen knives
have we no more than that which happens?

There are paths which have left behind no odor of life.

The city   was it a phantasm   erotically believed?

Read the wind   dream a sleep of unknowing   lie down
with the Noonday Demon.

History

The dead, what can they lift?
They can be let go.

Was there a bridge passed over?
I did not notice it.

A shopping bag of absence
is carried home.

■

The dead, what do they hear,
a fearful nothing?

Or is it our twittering cries
that go unheard?

Our birdsong complaint
without answer.

■

The dead, a haze at sunrise,
an atmosphere.

They have a way of being
here in my breath,

Yet unclear in the glaze
of memory

■

The dead, they live in the words
I say to them.

They reply in my words only,
in family talk.

Socrates, do you recall
smalltalk?

Columbia 1960

It seems to me that the new poem will not come out of the soul's loneliness, but rather out of a concern for language: i.e. what can be said that will not lead us into the same alienation that our previous language—the whole store of images that we call civilization—has produced for us. It will not be a poem of idealism or separation and longing. Rather, it will be a series of propositions whose ambiguity will produce, not alienation, but a kind of attention which can only be called mystical, which is to say, not reducible to logical form or language as a tool of logic.

It once was that in speaking we assumed that we were speaking of something objectively there in the real world. We then presumed to know the world in speaking of it. We assumed we could change and improve the "state of affairs" of the world.

Tell me now in your own words, "What happened?"

Ten Philosophical Asides

467.   I am sitting with a philosopher in the garden; he says again and again "I know that's a tree," pointing to a tree that is near us. Someone else arrives and hears this, and I tell him, "This fellow isn't insane. We are only doing philosophy."

LUDWIG WITTGENSTEIN, *On Certainty*

I.

2.   From its seeming to me—or to everyone else—to be so,
it doesn't follow that it is so.

We can ask and
in the asking   doubt
finds its ground

the proposition itself
is questioned   the red
leaf I have brought
indoors to say it is
autumn   dries before us

the red   changing   less red
leaf is no proof at last

we are alone again   doubt
and silence hold the ground.

II.

8. The difference between the concept of 'knowing'
and the concept of 'being certain' isn't of any great
importance at all, except where 'I know' is meant
to mean I can't be wrong.

At random   aspen leaves
spot fire the evergreen
outside my window.

Inside my eyes   that's
where the spears are thrown.

Yellow blades on the dark
green needles of pine.

Sun-struck bronze
of Hammurabi's legions
soon to be blood-tipped.

How may I be wrong and
at random   say   'I know'
as the wars go on?

III.

33.   Thus we expunge the sentences that don't get us any further.

Surf backs into ocean
after breaking bones.

A tone of voice
foams into rocks.

Sound fulfills laws

Silver sheathing tricks
illusions of surfaces
illusions of silver depths
all law bound   formal
as an ocean of lies.

What point have we
reached   is there any
place else to go?

In what manner of
speaking   may I ask?

IV.

63.   If we imagine the facts otherwise than they are,
certain language games lose some of their importance,
while others become more important. And in this way
there is an alteration—a gradual one—in the use
of the vocabulary of a language.

It is October and
rabbits fly amidst
rising autumn leaves.

The lake makes a statement.

I (the I is not important)
have never set foot
on the moon.
        Some things
are taken for granted.

Of course he is who
he says he is. I can
tell by his necktie.

V.

141.   When we first begin to believe anything, what we
believe is not a single proposition, it is a whole
system of propositions. (Light dawns gradually
over the whole.)

Once only   under a rising
illusionist moon   ethereal
presences   traceries   of a face

body parts plain   more
odorous than photographs
or telephones   slowly connecting

explicit parts   revealing
names   the sum of which   the
names of things   wastes away as

light dawns gradually over the whole.

VI.

229.   Our talk gets its meaning from the rest of our proceedings.

Because it happened   I say
a dog barking means
the end of the world   I say
this is the way it is
and then a dog barks
and what I believe unravels
within me and the shell
of the world echoes the barking
of dogs   because it happened
this is the way it is   I say
it may happen again.

VII.

410.   Our knowledge forms an enormous system. And only
within this system has a particular bit the value we give it.

That tree is wise
that does not up
and walk away.

True to the value
given it
it bends and sways.

One step
over the line
and we are stopped
forever in silence.

No matter that
the mountains march
into the sea.

VIII.

442.   For may it not happen that I imagine myself
to know something?

Imagine the pieces
whole again   fact
and odds and ends

ends beyond means

a landscape with clear
features   except nothing
to know   valley and plain

silence against silence

sound empties the ears

unlocatable pain.

IX.

454.   There are cases where doubt is reasonable,
but others where it seems logically impossible.
And there seems to be no clear boundary
between them.

Like missed baggage we sit
in places that have names
unknown to our claimants
who fret in other places
at speeds and pressures
that split all things apart
a condition necessary
perhaps   to the birthing of stars
but fatal   to simple pairing
necessary to recognition
and the claiming of our own.

X.

559.   You must bear in mind that the language game
is so to say something unpredictable. I mean: it
is not based on grounds. It is not reasonable
(nor unreasonable).

It is simply there—like our life.

Whatever it is   there it is
bent beneath the full burden
of a life   our language
carries us   we are born
to the equation   both sides
equal   these words   these
vows   this rising-falling breath.

Marginalia: Whitehead

"The notions of the Past and Future are then ghosts within the
face of the Present."

                              Boredom
is the result   neverending creation

                              Creation
is like   you know   breath
                              Instead
may I recall the painful wastes of the past
and anticipate death   shrive the present
with a backward glance
                              Suffer vision

                              Ghosts
attend me   that I may remain human
to the end.

                    Columbia 1960

Quotations

1.

Logic of properties,
hieroglyphics of logical
situations are, of necessity
true, although independent
of falsehood or truth.

Thus, in speaking the truth,
"A world is, as it were,
put together experimentally."

2.

At the very least, we
represent a relation. We are,
put this way, "On good ground."

3.

Once again
it all makes sense
except where we have not
given meaning
to what appears
to be a word.

"Even when we believe
we have done so."

To be ambiguous
would be to run on
forever. Simplicities
are enormously
complex. Consider
the sentence "I love
you."

It can be said
to be good without
knowing whether it
is false or true.

Columbia 1960

Analects

The ragman's cry   echo   from a boarded well
summoned out of death   crumbs from the table

■

an exquisite black page

■

armadas of significance   always offshore
hindsight flotillas
all this to contemplate   when impulse overflows
and spills the acids of memory
the past drains meaning away from death

a perfected puzzle   unassembled.

■

as if names equal shapes and area
or the last call before the joint closes

the sillier this gets the closer it comes to the flame.

■

speak as if to children or to god

the most primitive requests

hands-on presence of the dead is not
of their doing   it is we who remember

whispers   from the library of promises
other narrators   time's rungless ladder

pure nonsense of the numinous

■

a fantasy that language follows the world
drawn shutters against a sunset in the east
and the exit of words

come trembling to the place where the path
breaks off   when the pounding stops or leaps off
to a vanishing uncountable counter rhythm

no record of (can this be called an event)? survives.

■

uncertainty of a labyrinth and the way to go
balance is at issue   "color within the lines"

and the way to the center shall lead away
from the illusion that there is light at the center

or that the center is a place to be found

by walking a path that leads to a center

stilt walking   on cobblestones   life-
long corrections   that breath requires.

from d e l e t e

I.

Priced to ease pain and drain despair away, this made-up thing, trip-trap world, theme park. Jammed brain circuits flop like newspapers on New York Sunday streets. There! Who hurries into the underground headed uptown where the wish to be rid of all bone-weight steeps in a tea dish? There were dainty sandwiches one summer, our love's ache, edible, put to the teeth, opera on the radio, the playoffs on TV. Like any person in the room, tree-bending winds invite our agonies, we might as well forget our own salvation, we weren't made for it anyway, but don't ask for the where or the why of it, I wasn't going your way anyhow, not now at least. We live for the counteractual, my fox, admit it, carry for a while this bucket of lies. For your ears only, rumors are spread on the cobbled streets where Sunday papers dance. Not a column inch can do you in, saccharin are the sins of yesterworld. If you really cared, whose head would turn and smile? When did you think that last mile worth walking? Watch out for objects bearing compassion, thugs at heart, and humming with drugs of the tango. Oh, little one, sleep! If you must know, scissors and rock, how it all comes out, boot it up and be done with it, otherwise the game will crash, with nothing for anyone to do except go home. The pendulum, old hypnotizer, breathes with grief, numb any part you wish, this needle will not hurt your tale. So tell me now what time you keep, what tick or tuck or tiddly matters. Write what you will, these walls will never show up in court, so forget it, being there I mean. You are already taxied wildly away. Hang on, hang on as if your life depends on it, as it does, it's just rain on the roof, unreal illumination that comes before thunder, there's no ontology in that, just noise. Make the most of your off-the-rack walk, try to remember you were hung there in hope, threadbare some people might say. Focus. Focus. Public and private speech: do the State's service or be done unto. The difference between window dressing and window shopping is the subject of the last book you read. It equals being bothered or what you bother with. Look to the weather with nothing to taste. Hope, perennial death ship orbiting the sun. The offshore cloud bank will make shore by night. Ho!

2.

Set up curbside, jewelry tray entanglement with things looking up, but nothing sells unless there is someone looking down, and who might that be? For the moment it's not raining and off-coast in pods the gray whales parade south. Photographs sprout with the season. The gray whale's spout is heart shaped, enough said. Just listen for the icon's intake of breath and see what you can see. Yes, but that was yesterday and which way are prices going to go? There is a pack forming and they will need a leader. It's then you kick the snot out of them, not before, and make it believable this one last time; but don't depend on it, auditors, even though it's turned out like this so many times before. There may be an image whose mind has changed. Sorry, no rain checks in this scheme of things, the windows are broken and boards keep out the light, it's the cheapest thing to do and then forget it, as has been done before, before, etc. Could you pick out of a lineup who is the culprit here? The mirror is one-way and there's no way to be sure which side you're on, but so what? Go on making faces anyway, but be sure, now and then, to check your hand before your face, if just to say Wheaties, the best is yet to be. Our inventions, god and needles, for instance, are built to say this to us ever and forever. It's obvious why we can't give them up, they're ours, for ourself self's sake! We live in the afterlife of what, unalterable, has already taken place. The minute you start acting like Robinson Crusoe it's plain to see you've lost your hold on the world. There are many such, so many, washed up on our island shores! They end up sleeping over grates and in doorways at night, far distant from tree ripe fruit and warm sand. The dumps of our artifacts bewilder them. They probe, not knowing what to expect from excess. They act out an experiment, a hairline calculation for survival: is the expenditure of energy to dig up carrots from the frozen ground more than their return in calories? Did you notice the price tag when the wine was poured, the cool chardonnay, the special cabernet, white and red absurdities of words? The motion lights are set to react outside the house but, tell me, did you see the clutter in the study, one would think! Those catalogs, the cave, shadows.

3.

Once again, flannel on the lawn at dawn. Threats of purgatory rising with the sun. Why so early, double? There are pros who play this sport for blood, yours will do. Edges of sardine cans await your hands. Caution is not the question, the question is who will be the last to be asked to dance! Watch out for the glare ice there ahead. Do not touch the brakes or the whole gazebo will go flying into the sunrise, late for school, yesterday's uniform still unpressed and soiled. Stay on the phone, at least until you hear the beep, be sure to have your message ready, helpless, the oars have been left behind, the stars not out, invisible in chill cloudcover, it's damn cold out here in the open tonight, no spooky moonglade to glide upon and sleep. And whose intention this morning is it to hang the jury before lunchbreak and jump ahead to night, armed with a chic and veiled beginning, or to try another channel in seriousness meaning now, today, remotely, but forever. Right there, with the questions unanswered, is where reality begins and ends and may well have been over before. Your turn next in the yard may come, make the most of it, keep those buttocks tight, chin up for class and country, the old home town. Yes. Like a god of legend, of a far distant time, and it isn't a matter of like, it's more a question of packaging and shelf life, a plea bargain is always possible, assuming you can hold yourself together in the soup for a whole day and night, and then show up on the lawn again, fresh-faced and vulnerable. Remember, there is no one minding the store. What store? Oh, just an expression they will use rounding any corner, drenched and testy with the accumulated facts of life. Pretend not to notice that the Big Game is over, that the "masses" have been moving away from home, except for the usual freeway snarls. Why doesn't somebody say "There's nobody here but us neutrals?" Which is not to say it is unnatural, only that it is nowhere to be found in nature, invented as we go along. But enough about you, a flame-orange sun does not (be sure you have enough OJ for breakfast) boil the cold Pacific, not yet. Also, before birth, before death from the common air, first cry, you should know this is a licensed no-host bar. Ohno!

4.

You mean that? History? This traffic is history, it's speed. Forget
about crossing the street, you'll get run over, like how far can the
slow-pitch softball of sentience reach? Come on now! Over the
plate, pretend you can bash it into realms of unbeing, it's a game
mon frère, the pitch and the hit must coexist, it's in the rules, and it's
your only chance of making do, but remember, be careful where
you're pointing, there may be words hidden in corners, birds of a
sort in any weather, morning may find that "you" did it, the rib-bitt
merely of a literary frog. Each generation a box with all the pieces
is handed down. Spread out on the table under lamp light each year
the picture has more holes in it, don't look under the bed, can you
imagine anyone mothering you with your history? Suppose you
were to blow the whistle, spill the beans, would anyone applaud,
could anyone bear to have your name in gold on the party list?
That's just the way it goes, and you'll miss those fat pitches or look
the other way as a strike sails by. It's the rules again, stupid (lie and
let lie), and all that slamming, bamming, and, yes, breath-held
hullabaloo of love is history's traffic come to run you down. As if
history is apart from something you did, you son of a bitch. Too
late now for any midcourse corrections, midtown erections, the
skyline is too crowded, besides, you'd never make it through the
maze to a deconstruction permit. "Waltz . . . Ladies and
Gentlemen, if you please" . . . the Viennese, that waltz of history,
gentility's fiction and reflection from the polished ballroom floor.
Should the conscience of the race belong to women? Some man is
always cutting in and cries of conscience, conscience in the night are, to
most ears, silent, silent as the great owl's flight. The kill is never

clean, but if you must know, little brother, know that only you can
claim that nature or an owl can care. Invention is your signature,
your worth, the bliss of nature is anything but that, no pastures
where poets may safely graze or kill, believe in Holy Name and
Cause. That's a nasty trick you have Saint Augustine, hysterical
logician, "from weakness to habit to necessity." But, seriously
speaking, your subscription will expire in three months, so respond,
respond, please mail now. Yes. Be an early bird and save.

5.

The pea beneath my mattress, my prince, is you. Don't ask, you
may be forgiven whatever offenses may be yours, and that paper
moon may be a map of your mind, the sweet ache of a sky-blue
day. Please learn not to depend on schedules as printed, deadlines
are months ahead of every event. So gallop about as if your life is
real as that jagged Matterhorn in Anaheim, forgive the local
reference, so much of what you think you see flies by you truly
undetected, you're in a soup which, once again, you have mistaken
for perfect vision. The pollution of old Pittsburgh has moved to
Beijing, and speaking of being, as you say you were, behold an
empty hand, a peace offering from the undersecretary whose eyes
never once sought yours. It pours, it pours, when it's not raining
tears, sentiment so thick you think you'll choke, but why not go for
broke, head into the worst of it, a survivor setting off for help.
Frostbite is common, keep moving if you can, look for landmarks
you may have passed before. The trouble is, it all changes with
light, no place to lie down, rest, or even weep. The best, there is proof,
get run over in the sand, better to find a clan, a tribe, a gang—not

likely for the old imperial you—you moved into civilization, remember? You can't be a one-man fortress, comrades in arms have deserted, been executed as is the style today. That necklace of fire, the mind vomits it! A song sparrow sings in the brush, and in the firs the ruby kinglets' chatter fills each tree. You have yet to try on language for size, some day, after the ugly swelling has gone down, if clan and all the rest fails, try religion, not one that from a high pulpit blesses war, try one that fights, Pentecostal say, or one that sanctions a holy war for an underclass. Otherwise, put on your grandfather's old pith helmet, look ridiculous, and become a sniper's perfect target. After all, indeterminacy is on your side, you could emerge as one more god, the man who orders milkshakes for all the neighborhood kids. Meanwhile, cast your vote into the lake, pretend not to notice that the women have left town, it's eerie, you can't disagree with that. Send out as many thank you notes as you have cards. The pink ones? Well, no point in those. It's the mailbox, not the government, that won't swallow them.

6.

Assume you have discovered an entropy of spirit, immeasurable of course, but it pulls graveward all those whose element is breath, not as the in and out again of water and the sun, but oblivion's ass-first downhill twenty-four-hour drag. Knowledge is an after-the-fact affair, fair game for a hunger striker's skeptic gopher tooth. Remember your "agenbite of inwit," but don't, please don't, go knocking on doors declaring you've gone hollow with all the others, no one will believe you so long as your bag of flesh is fair. Fall down the stairs to another street. Have you noticed nature does not care for you, no matter the pathos of your fallacies, your antiperspirant, or your arms folded over the stretch marks of your hardest years? That's you, cell mate, roping a Platonic calf. Rare air, this is all you'll catch and never can. Live on that for a week and leave a message on your machine, "nourished by words alone." Those fireworks you inherited, where are they now? Will you set them off to end the show? You have a story that simply cannot be sold, and no rewrite can change country or cast, so here you are in never-never land again. That figure off there in the mist is Nietzsche, stay clear, they say his breath is vile, he needs his space or so the professors say. Were you handed this out of an old script or are you improvising this to-do? Whatever you are, an actor or a human merely with all the other actors, or can you tell the difference without a script in hand, you talk about a text that is not there. Each morning your own short-form obituary appears on every page. An open mike will follow. But this is only in the babblesphere, don't inhale those dialogues that bubble up. Weariness grows in direct proportion to answers that recede nightly as you snore. Did you audition for this part or did you win it in an all-night poker game? The difference is the same, none, today. Don't give your chips to another to bet, that's stacking the odds in your favor, sharing the blame. Avoid places where the lights are always on. Try finding a sunset through a simple gift of looking west. There can be too much light for your own good. Pace Pascal. Let someone close your eyes. Necessary, or so I'm told. That hand in front of your face, try it now.

"Come Live with Me"

"A swan in the ice of its own disposition"
The phrase is Giorgio's
The absence is my own
difficult to detect
as astral matter in the flux of disappearance.

Did any of this happen and
if so is there more to say? Yes.

"From desire to mourning"
Giorgio again
guest of the rose   ice block of metaphor
dissociation from love's signature
renunciation by way of recovery.

Just a suggestion
the rule box is not open   not yet

Keening is ancient   uncalculated and chill
expectation is our only fixed illusion
imagine an opposite   it would be unbearable
there is no cause greater or lesser than
cause and place as ever and ever one.

: It :

Time was. There is now a different measurement in place.
It has more to do with endurance than dimension,
a property of stasis with people, animals, and wind rushing past. It is
a watershed from which all things rush away.
There is no becoming, destinations have been proved absurd.
It is a game of propositions: it is this: this is it:
it is nothing: it is being   :   poised:
the *it* comes loose from reference and has elsewhere to go.

from Writing the Silences

I.

Let us consider	the cat's pajamas
an unfocused	word sieve
a wordless Plato	a wish
to live	I think
a word I	the appearance of
is enough	to shrink the world
there will be	no coffee
following silence	no
metaphor	the lies
language	tells itself
mind's random	storms
calms	a climate
¡Mira!	the moon
Hail!	passerby
inbeing	how goes
the night	the the

2.

An itch	god is not
elsewise inevitable	faith
truckstop cry	"O rocks!"
unlocatable memory	limitless in night
memory	an infection
in air	wind borne
skunk odor	days after
the barely discernible	road kill
Orpheus	(re)membered
flawed	with parts missing

3.

Permission to be	what no longer
I am	will never be
waterfall	at speed
unpointable	ideal mere
those are real	gunshots not
a machine to scare	birds from a field
dead before hitting	real earth
Dr. Johnson's	pointed boot
never a matter	of again
unrecognizable present	: in theory
dislocated	head-figure
in a photograph	moving
silver gelatin	unfixed
evident ever	afloat

4.

More or less   yes
along   along for sure

a fire affair   error
animal   liar   liar

lacking a   that which
is not   as if

ecosophical   rats in the wall
follow a dot   is to follow a line

stay in line   for Pascal's case
a case surely   a waste only after

not thought   experiment
nor any   referent

no bringing to focus   night's sieve
imprecision of   atomic measurement

dogma   illusion's glove
let fall all   junctures down

5.

Avalanche
a field

the broken wave
mansions

mushrooms
unlikeness

a safe where
land of

ladders without
a finite forever

go figure
flop

principle
ditch

an apropos
dig to

underspace
runabout

overhigh
walkover

scales
random given

(mal)adjusted
from

6.

Well enough	unstrung
footfall	follow through
shall we now	they go
into return	nightlife
shallow depths	edgewild
never about	as such
nor here	again
base	meant
breakwater	golden
deepskin	fallow

7.

The skin	past of
zero	without which
noplace	sand base
towers	a pre-proposition
by grain by	a number
Danae	rape
gold	nonstandard
nausea	truth of
of when	then who
but how	off it
neverno	westward
nose	sphinx missing

8.

Don't look hereinfor	vision of one
general idea of	the whole
completeness or union	by any means
it is not easy	to give up
religious unrealities	behold the chain
of burned utopias	back within sight
a burning bush	grail quest
in default	words gone rotten
a little like Schoenberg	the question "why?"
may bring it off	only tonalities in time

"Come Sunday"

With God passed out
of this galaxy
Rilke's angels have come down—
an unrepeatable effect—in flames

the old convenience stops
adoration stations are bankrupt
their roofs open to the rain
where have you been

it is dangerous to be out
there are lonely snipers
in the ruined spires

Birthright

I.

That which there is to speak of, to make as it were like creation, a test of novelty, with infinite failure, a daily undoing. We are delivered into beginning, our evolutionary résumé writ large in a travel case of mortal selves. Motion is within afterthought, within time as measured amid knickknack shelves of a life's attachment. Desire is a prerequisite of being: odor of cellars forever damp, erotic; a something before, unpredictable and not a bit an idle matter.

II.

No exceptions. Lapsed into a country of foreclosure, that which calls back becoming, infinite regress into a wish not to be born, not to have been selfish, and with an ego on the way. Nonentity which loves, self-like in sleep, in other events entangled, fallen away—but from where? It is the most human power: to not be.

III.

What color will flowers and thorns take tomorrow here where the here and the there may be the same? Words, tablets of stone, a child must bear them, playing all parts in the unity of whatever can be said, an environment, a house of flash cards, blinding illumination of signs, genetic grammar before a hurricane but it passes and is rebuilt in the new neighborhood and the same process except the out-there becomes the other, split from head to toe. And whatever grief befalls, you know you did it somehow, being born.

IV.

It is the same language, but it is not the same. Overnight, words gone adrift, prosperity in common language becomes depression. Come now to speak of it, to pick out from the stadium of words that have been said, the self-defining scattershot story of free choice irreproachable with truth, born tired into limbo America, not guilty for not having lived it through.

V.

To build empires, ideologies of race, and desperate traveling salesmen, brittle words out of the family plot, they will crack. We will always have among us the forever inarticulate, shocked speechless after a War, a '29 Crash. There are those who will start again and again and alone, and there are those who will wait for War to come in their time. The red solution, its elixir, so much in afterthought, wild-eyed ignorance. I recall how the mills blazed, poured red and green currencies, prosperity afire. A generation of patriots: volunteer, object with conscience, with religion, or play the lottery. I will not give the one freedom I have, my so-called arm and mind, to the State. The lack of perception of evil is no excuse, ignorance once again. No one wins, but there are losses beyond biblical comprehension. Randolph Bourne: "War is the health of the state." Afterthought again.

VI.

Form to be filled or circumstance to be met. Can this be called a happy history? Completed, unannounced, unfelt, words accumulate a toolbox of deceits, stories sawed and hammered to fit, how we explain ourselves to ourselves, world to world. "Sign here! or forfeit your lady, your lands, your lunatic loves." A voice from long ago sang low. "That's love," so sang the radio.

VII.

On the headland meadow, unexpected, two larks untangle song above October grass. Glorious here: not here, taken by language, built-in in language, a seasonal carnival of signs, mock images, again ended upon exit and absence, even of absence, not in the word.

VIII.

For each singularity, a War tattoo, indelible. Early in the century's fifth decade I was called. *Psychotic neurotic.* Artsy freak. Is there that which is in between origins and what happens, before the origins of the ten thousand things, before? There is no greening nor return, no spring forward in time regardless of sweat, blood and the afterthought of tears. In a field of uncommonness words become investigative only, commerce is paltry, animals make stern demands, but wait; there are landslides closing off the common retreats to the expressible. "Here we are," say the transients in the ice palace of old age, but they rush away, perhaps to other rooms, mumbling their scenes. In snowfall each crystal is an absolute judgment, moment by moment, of a life. The flakes melt upon contact, as between sleep and waking the weight is upon sleep. Caligari's somnambule steps nightly into me. The first and last charge upon life: to resist bad dreams, to hold ground under the lifelong tenebrous scald of love.

Notebook

Diagnosis: *weakening neuromodulatory control.*

A trapeze flyer's grasp of the bar
not that easy   of course I'll fall

passing through fractured light
a galactic separation throws me away

I have never been so far from home

This Morning

madness crept into my pocket
like a hairy bug

I cannot say I saw it
but I believe it
to be there   waiting

how move without moving?
remember   without despair?

I pray the wind shall not
rise up and wrap about me

I hold out my hands in balance
a dancer preparing to move.

Aftershock

Afterward, you look on the world as a happy place
flush from arrival into a new land of not being in pain.
Is there anything forgotten, now that the screaming's stopped?

The voltage doctor has put upon you a happy face.

Coffee stains come and go, echoechoecho.
This can be validated, the night crew cleans up.

A gurney wheels you to damnation sedated, but somebody
pushes . . . a body . . .

Name your place or person, it is not a freedom.

Serenity is unearthly,
the hospital staff tests you with the hammer of happiness,
we say each other's names, but also we remember,
we remember

it all : and nothing.

Visiting Hours

What we do is habit   or guesswork
                           unless otherwise
posted.

        ▪

I was given a time.

        ▪

A common house finch at the feeder is glorious in red.
In a quick breath between the storms the always happening is made
                           visible.
Plucked away and gone.
I shall try to remember that talisman finch.   Until then
things remain as they are as I present myself to a glass window
                           as to a shaving mirror.

        ▪

"Wait here. You will be let in."   Remembering
a pandora of oaths   in unexpected places
parts of an agon   a near murder: "This is it, DIE!"
Speeding toward a cliff edge, a child's scream, his life-plea, skids
through the gravel, hot metal, hot rubber, red mist in the eyes.

        ▪

Assassins wait to intercept a mumblin' word.

        ▪

It is not yet time, but there will be a time when light, like water,
                    must be fought for:
in order to see, in order to speak to the question:
                    "What have we here?"

Consciousness cannot live apart, we are in an area of propositional
uncertainty   chicken   egg   "Is there a family history?"

It is dangerous to make too much sense, even in science.

       ■

"Wait here. Someone will come for you."

There are no answers in this cabinet of magic
long ago   broken into   trashed   robbed.
                    Hush little baby.

       ■

"This way."

The room was locked.
A wire-glass window in the door was small.
There was no other.

A light bulb burned behind a grate in the ceiling.

Far from the dangerous utensils of home
my knee-hugging love
sat on the medicinal floor.

The Parachutist's Annunciation

Carried to term   it may be suicidal to know of it all there is.

Together we have eaten of the notorious unreliability of prediction.

The only way out is accident.

Someone has to jump or be pushed.
The descent is the same   the crushing weight of the ordinary.

There may be a taboo against dropping in this way
falling swiftly and unannounced with miracles on your tongue.

And to whom might we turn to unwind absurdity   only to spin again
who among us is faithful?

Heroes in body armor, dirt, and blood gather from far-off Fresno,
all the exotic countries of Europe.
                              Later, the also-rans will wait
as for Odysseus in bad faith or in terror—
                              whichever comes first in their story.

Umbrella   barn roof   haystack   a wish to be an angel
American Standard.

From two hundred feet up   a voice descending.
Obviously   the surprise is endless   "captured on film"
and there are issues that will never be settled.

                    Into the crowd, where?
                    No one could be sure.

The message was delivered before the infraction could be reported.

A crackle of a logo-covered unisex jumpsuit
caused us to look up   too late   we saw there is no time.

One message   like whales' dense force-fed milk   growth substance.

That knowledge!!!

Oh, to be fed on thistles   salt   the unshaded sun.

Holding On

I.

How account
for dimming
of the lights

baggage
of old age
tagged and waiting?

or light tricks
in snow
at sun-up?

waiting in line

waiting in line

come sundown
watching the horizon
eyes glowing.

2.

Who

not the
other myself
my prisoner

night flesh
ear-skewered

music
in natural
air

screams   well-deep
seep to the brain-root

days
Treblinka nights

guilt
guts the ferret
in my cage

sanity puddles the floor.

3.

In memory sickness

eyes unlace

open
as last night's boots

a glacier of light
saps the air

remember

the torturer's
tinnitus
starts the day.

4.

The   irrationality
of it

mob noise

angels struck
from the block
of darkness

a sunlit sky breaks
through in shrapnel

hard screaming night

feather touch

troops improvising
for the kill

panic

my enemy

my nail-hold.

5.

Of the texture
of elbows shattered
and stairwell falls

hallucinations
of confession

rush to stop pain.

6.

Andean snow-stars
blind me

the flashlight
of the Burglar
of Death flares

and holds
on my eyes.

7.

In the Feast Halls

ghosts linger

feeding

avoiding

dogs

and the memory

of cracked bones.

8.

Present danger

colors hiss
from a blue masque

bone-bonded

Autumn in no
year's season

a nerve twitches
across the path.

9.

Planets by lamplight

street laughter
embraced in being

parallel lines
collapse curbside

cornices fall

from a stranger's dream
moon-sand ears

the inhabitants
lean in to hear.

. . . a divertimento . . .

My metaphysical coyotes have pissed off and gone.
I was Edmund's therapist while Lear looked on and howled.
I am from Cherry Street on a wedding anniversary, a tenth-year mistake.
I have logged my fourscore and there is a Model T in my head.
My prayer mat is a satellite circling a fire-prone planet.

I have seen the icons of poetry step down from their frames and deflate
I have felt the finger cymbals of Kali seduce me toward death.
I have been reborn with Elizabeth Bishop's disasters in my lap
I have heard States and the holders of power sing the same song:
"Come, dilly, dilly, come and be killed."

I have knelt in the four dusty corners of my life and have been shown
the bloody hands of the Keepers of the Promised Land.

I have seen enough to last for the life of a sparrow

Footnotes

1. The ownmost possibility of the day
   is to die   it is a burden
   heavy coins on the eyelids upon waking.

2. Approaching a final disclosure (nothingness)
   there is an increase in the enclosuring (hiddenness)
   of all things (matters that pertain to life).

3. Phantoms
   those train conductors
   pay no attention
   to what the living say
   but they talk to us
   incessantly.

4. My metaphysical coyotes have pissed off and gone,
   there are none to keep me once this complaint is done.

5. A delusion of kitchen knives and photographs
   complete with stormhowling winds unseemly jinns.

6. A lasting consolation is
   that through all this wasted time
   I've not stopped dying.

7. Overheard dialogue: "She's remembering what never happened."
   Response: "Yes, if you don't value reality it goes away on you."

8. Death asks no questions
   nor is history a continued story

9. Who decided: "Let's have a touchstone for reality"?
   Oh Liar. Liar.

10. It is life that kills.
    Death eludes wisdom
    and never fails.

11. Death is untouchable
    language cannot reach it
    life reaches it but once.

12. Whence comes the faith
    that we may find what we are looking for?

13. There has not been time to recover from culture.

14. In the seeming interior of the mind
    there is no map   no dialogue
    merely bowling ball interior gutter noise.

15. My poems represent another probe
    into the uncertainty of language
    within the killing task of life.
    "Do you tell me that now?"

16. Suicide   suicide is the talk in the room.
    It lies dark in the corners and twists
    around chairs and tables like smoke.

17. Roots are an impediment to mobility.

18. The erotic world is still the erotic world
    with the everready batteries of youth.

19. *"I do in troth."*

A Funeral of Memory

Immaculately buried memory sets
unworkable as past life   retrievable at will

thinking of god   I draw a blank

I say "Enter, thin needle of infinite night."
and so it is   the set is overfull

calling on god   I enter the set called silence

once in the labyrinth   old alley of no exit
there is only the center and the deception of place
here everything happens and nothing is foretold

listening for god   I hear my footsteps vanishing

living in silence   I recall what I cannot hear.

The Winter Garden

"A sad tale's best for winter."
MAMILLIUS in *The Winter's Tale*

1.

Parasite in the muscled body of power
Glutted on a bloody century past

Out of action   marking slow time
Waiting for sundown   leaning from the past

Garden Inventory—A

Copenhagen Cabbage   Kale
Plum Purple Radish   Bell Beans
Goldmine Carrot   Red Romaine
Triple Curled Parsley   Chard
Collard Greens   Crisphead Lettuce
Chicory   Tatsoi   Pok Choi
Early Italian Purple
Garlic   Little Marvel Peas

2.

Once born
look   eventually
into where from

scars of a world's waste
trenches full of winter

scum water   nothing detectable
in snowfall
break the ice

men lived here
No, men died here

Garden Inventory—B

  Italian Parsley

  Oregon Snow Peas

  Brussels Sprouts   Mustard

  Rhubarb   Kohlrabi

  White Lisbon Scallions

  Early Wonder Beets

      3.

Five hundred
Eighty-five
Thousand between
Late July rains
And early
November snow

Passchendaele
Sorrow in the saying

Garden Inventory—C

Oriental Cabbage
Butterhead Lettuce   Squash
Utah Yellow Onions
Potatoes   Bright Lights Chard

4.

Mud buried
Blood slumber

Garden of white
Crosses   file tabs
Of ghosts   ghastly
Harvest of ignorance
Senile pride

There are ways of being that leave no odor of life
many have passed down this stone road unnumbered

Garden Inventory—D

Swiss Chard

Spinach

Clover

Lettuce

Onions

Fava Beans

Garden Inventory—E

Beets

5.

Perspective
Technical
Geometric
Atmospheric
Illusion
Engineering
Illusion
Wall shadows
The cave story
Believe it
What looks real

The ritual says itself
there is no theory of living
our language
makes sense if living makes sense

Find the future in a nest of nerves
phoenix or viper   time has outstepped time

static in the one dimension that remains

step with pockets of stone into a flood
and freeze the hot and onward rushing blood
stop cold the knee joints' and the world's pains

dismantle history's theoretic spine
with life the issue   guess what hinders and what serves

turn inside out and outside in
abandon the cellular palace of the skin
blown to bits or spotted with old age

force together peace and humankind
in an exploded classroom of the mind

speak of resurrection and of ruin
in a battlefield with shot down angels strewn

amid   wind flattened scarecrows   words on a page
all desolation's patronage

A Treasury of Darkness

It is necessary to begin in obscurity because shadow
which lives by light is obscure   yes because
but not by cause   a wholly realized worldly event

not unlike an upside-down mountain in a lake
which is a different event and casts no shadow
and is likely to last as long as an afternoon

the value of shadow is what it does and therefore is
it can be spoken of as *doppelganging* to an abstract degree
the suspicious gerund pretending to be the object which the shadow is

of the other which carves light in its course we are talking somewhere
around a world of which there is no other of its class apart from this present
flat black and white shadow of a green and brown frond of palm

which is not simply a palm frond this cannot be a shadow speaking
the shadow which would not be here except for light and the living
palm   are there other claims to be made of this event?   Yes—

Introit

Texts speak of a light stronger than all others   unbearable
light that grinds light of our best efforts to invisible darkness
palm is shade between saving or killing light   choose all texts with care

into a journey however it may be put   in whatever vehicle
soul or embodied mind or body and mind or again whatever vehicle
of suffering in whatever receptacle of suffering without limit or will

shall we speak of pure mind only to know it ends when the circuits shut
    down
of course we can't be sure that this may or not be the point   :   run that
by me again brainy gang banger   thinking to get out with the lights

still on the digital   choice not made   better still   never made
except in ritual which leaves the lights on and the words spoken.

Over the Shoulder

Looking back it must be said the labels have changed
futures have no translatable script
the common serenity of language has been jigsawed
it is how life as lived—is lived—.

Fiction's pretense is to absolutes—they are what they are—
nothing undergoes change—of course—that's how it is.

In February dry leaves rattle in the London plane trees of Claremont
there is a circle around the moon—which circles on and on—
the leaves twirl Viconian spirals as they fall
the dog is unwilling to return but the leash holds
—ostensive definition—a porch light says I am headed—there.

Meanwhile

Memory   discontinuous
as rain

a sustenance not of history
nor of any common nourishment

momentary presences of worlds
efficient cause   lifelasting effort

to leave on life the lightest imprint.

POEMS 1946–1957

from A History Primer

The seasons change and the red vines burn on the hillside.
The vines are red where refugees again stare at the strange towns.
The seas are not yet bombed from their great basins, the people persist.

The human event, the fate, the fear remain predictable
Only in the most general of generalities, like seasons.
The wind is up and sand covers the suburbs of the cities.

We have counted the number of days by the dead, one death for every day.
It is, perhaps, that time passes through us like a winter's wind,
Leaving us raw, root-shaken, holding to hysteria as mistress
Of that gray field we wake to every day. We wake with weeping.

Move on. Hurry. Already the familiar has become as another country.

Hurry. In the failing light our weakeyed watches lose their sight.

Quick. Quick. Draw up the drowned straw god from the blue Phoenician sea.

Move on. From room to room. From chaos to chaos to chaos

To complete illusion, of partial beauty, of partial resurrection,

At last, in the slow, heavy, lovely, image-riddled mind.

1946

Seascape

The fishermen
are hauling on their nets for nothing;
their hands, quicker than spiders,
are among the copper cords,
the blue sea-bottles,
and their eyes
are pressed into a green wind.

The fishermen
are dragging the bay for monsters;
they are caging the waves for demons,
for sea-girls
and the deep down drag of love.

The nets are in the water,
they are heavy with silver in the onyx water.

The fishermen
are hauling on their nets for fish:
and one sees the eyes of his father
in a bearded wave,
and some watch the islands
rounding out of the water like breasts
or the curved belly of love.

1948

from September Elegy

Falls, in a wind-swirl, a spiral,
the ruddy leaf;
time's whirlpool turns us home,

turns,
high on the lifting thermals,
a slim hawk,
the wing tips keep
bold balance on the blind
push of air.

How far, how far
has the year turned,
time's long descending spiral
and the upward curl and push
of the living thing:

how deep
and in what distant journey
the late year wheels.

1948

from At Caesar's Gate

Time is a word order
a consistent convention
it is a word order
a hypothetical construction
an order of words
and numbers speaking
to the matter of time.

Before Christ and After
Death   this is a calendar
a rule which is not time
but a way of seeing
a minority view in all
but imperial power
Caesar's force of arms
at this century's end.

Nine centuries before Christ
Ashurnasipal II:
                    "I built a pillar
over against his city gate
and I flayed all the chief men . . .
and I covered the pillar with their skins . . .
their young men and maidens
I burned in the fire."
                    Post Holocaust:
victories are celebrated without
body counts   refugees are out of policy
bodies are piled by the blood spattered
Gate

■

We are   without choice   units
within the "history" of our time
not part of a chain   not one link
not even a nanosecond within
our own reckoning of time

The real and the absolute
are recognized within the life span
and in the residual work   neither
can pick its time   nor endure within
that artifice of time as a point of view

The residue is another history
a history of cruelty hypothesized
within a gridlock of time
and artifacts that crumble
like ourselves   to sand and grit

■

The "historicizer" stands
contingently
in a history
which is to say
in the darkness of time
not as a great abstraction
but as the only ground
for saying anything at all

I would be invisible in my cell.

1950

A Reminiscence

Held in a late season
At a shifting of worlds,
In the golden balance of autumn,
Out of love and reason

We made our peace;
Stood still in October
In the failing light and sought,
Each in the other, ease

And release from silence,
From the slow damnation
Of speech that is weak
And falls from silence.

In the October sun
By the green river we spoke,
Late in October, the leaves
Of the water maples had fallen.

But whatever we said
In the bright leaves was lost,
Quick as the leaf-fall,
Brittle and blood red.

For Kenneth Rexroth, 1950

Birthday View Opening on a Garden

Regardless of February and the usual rain
The overripe magnolias flaunt the wild weather;

White-pink, thick-leafed, the impossible magnolias
Giving in only to the strong wind at last

And lying there, too lush for the time of year,
They are balanced for the gardener's and the mind's sake

By the red flowering quince and Japanese plum
And by the evergreen rain in the winter trees.

The magnolias are sliced by the seasonal wind.
Like the fruits of our years, no power can hold them.

And the garden is all wreck, decay, and accident of weather,
Until a new largess of giving gives way in the mind

Like the wind sudden in the plum tree tearing
And covering everything, the storm, the hidden buds,
The slashed magnolias with a wild pink cloud.

For Thomas Parkinson, February 1957

Above: Richard Moore in front of shed, Duncans Mills, 1945.

Eleanor McKinney and Richard, Duncans Mills, 1946.

Top: Richard, Berkeley, 1954. Photo by Ida Mae Zapf.

Richard interviewing Stanley Kunitz, KQED, 1956. Photo by Richard Fowler.

Top: Richard interviewing Randall Jarrell, KQED, 1956. Photo by Richard Fowler.

Richard with Louis Zukofsky, New York, 1965. Photo by Phil Greene.

Above: Robert Creeley and Bobbie Ann Hawkins, New Mexico, 1965. Photo by Richard O. Moore.

Denise Levertov, New York, 1965. Photo by Richard O. Moore.

Top: Film crew, San Francisco, 1965. Left to right: Irving
Saraf (behind camera), Richard, Stanley Kronquest. Photo
by Ernest Lowe.

From left: Richard (back to camera), Aram Saroyan, Peter
Orlovsky with guitar, Allen Ginsberg, San Francisco, 1965.
Photo by Ernest Lowe.

Top: Anne Sexton with Richard, Boston, 1965. Photo by Stanley Kronquest.

Richard and family, Mill Valley, 1967. Left to right: Lisa, Aran, Richard, Ruth.

Top: Photo from a *Look* magazine profile of KQED, November 1970: Richard at Muir Beach with the staff of the experimental film series *The San Francisco Mix.*

Filming Ross Macdonald for the series *The Writer in America,* Santa Barbara, 1975. Left to right: Macdonald, Phil Greene, Richard, Susan Wengraf, Mark Berger. Photo by Charles Siddarth Kelly.

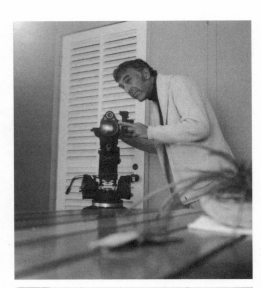

Top: Richard, Santa Barbara,
1975. Photo by Charles
Siddarth Kelly.

Robert Duncan,
San Francisco, 1975.
Photo by Richard O. Moore.

Richard O. Moore, Berkeley, 2009. Photo by Phil Greene.

Notes

"Dog in the Forest": In his book *Stanzas*, the contemporary Italian philosopher Giorgio Agamben recalls that in the Middle Ages the capital sin of sloth occasionally took the image of the noonday demon against which "the fathers exercised themselves with particular fervor."

"Ten Philosophical Asides": The quotations from Ludwig Wittgenstein are from the last year and a half of his life, following the publication of *Philosophical Investigations*. They were edited by G. E. M. Anscombe and G. H. von Wright and translated by Denis Paul and G. E. M. Anscombe. They were first published by Basil Blackwell in 1949 under the title *On Certainty*.

"Marginalia: Whitehead": In 1960 I received a CBS fellowship for a year's study at Columbia University. This allowed me to explore my interests in analytic and linguistic philosophy. "Quotations" and "Columbia 1960" are also from this time.

"'Come Live with Me'": Giorgio is Giorgio Agamben.

"'Come Sunday'": The title of a Duke Ellington work included in his Concert of Sacred Music. It was first performed at Grace Cathedral in San Francisco in 1965.

"The Parachutist's Annunciation": At the Fat Tire Bicycle Festival in Squaw Valley in 1997 I learned that the racers and stunt riders wore plastic armor. In the midst of the competition a parachutist (more accurately, a paraglider) descended without warning into the audience. The "annunciation" should be self-explanatory.

"Footnotes" 15 and 17: "Do you tell me that now" and "I do in troth" are from *Finnegans Wake*.

"A Reminiscence": This poem recalls walks with Kenneth Rexroth during visits with Eleanor McKinney and me at Duncans Mills, on the Russian River in Sonoma County, in the mid-1940s.

Designer *Claudia Smelser*   Text and Display *Garamond Premier Pro*
Compositor *BookMatters, Berkeley*   Printer *Maple-Vail Book Manufacturing Group*

∎